# Thinking in Poetry

*Stories from a Self Evolution*

Dr Katie Ellyn

Copyright © 2025 (Dr Katie Ellyn)
All rights reserved worldwide.

No part of the book may be copied or changed in any format, sold, or used in a way other than what is outlined in this book, under any circumstances, without the prior written permission of the publisher.

Inspiring Publishers
P.O. Box 159, Calwell, ACT Australia 2905
Email: publishaspg@gmail.com
http://www.inspiringpublishers.com

 A catalogue record for this book is available from the National Library of Australia

National Library of Australia The Prepublication Data Service

Author:   Dr Katie Ellyn
Title:    Thinking in Poetry: Stories from a Self Evolution
Genre:    Poetry
Website:  soulfiretherapy.com.au

Cover Artist: Arthur Dilly Muro

Paperback ISBN: 978-1-923449-63-3

Early poetry (phases 1 and 2) composed on Kuarna country.

Book compiled and written and most recent poetry (phase 3) composed on the land of the Ngunnawal and Ngambri people.

I wish to acknowledge the Traditional Custodians of the land and pay my respects to their Elders past and present. I acknowledge and respect their continuing culture and connection to land, waters, sky and community.

Sovereignty has never been ceded.

# Contents

Preface ................................................................... vii

Phase 1: Distortion ................................................... 1

Phase 2: Adaptation ................................................ 39

Phase 3: Activation ................................................. 57

# Preface

**Content Warning:** Self-harm, suicide, substance use, mental illness, abuse/neglect, death.

Please be aware that material in this book contains potentially triggering themes.

This book contains a compilation of poetry I have written over the course of my life. It evolved out of my efforts to reengage with what felt like a lost skill of expression through poetry. As I did so, I perceived such a stark contrast between my early poetry and my new compositions and felt a reflected inner evolution. 'Thinking in Poetry' is what I termed the practice I adopted to encourage my poetic creativity to reemerge.

I reflect on my teen years as a time of pain. I was physically and psychologically unwell. It was poorly understood and frequently dismissed, by both the medical establishment and friends and family. I eventually collected some labels; chronic fatigue, chronic depression, generalized anxiety. Years later, complex trauma.

For me, however, it was life as I knew it. I frequently felt suicidal. At some point I seemingly adopted the belief that it was normal and deserved that I be in such a state of pain that I wanted to die. I self-harmed and hid the cuts. I drank alcohol at times to alarming excess and used marijuana whenever I had the opportunity.

Yet I made the firm resolution with myself in those years to survive, no matter what. Along with my more maladaptive coping strategies, poetry was part of how I did that. I didn't call it anything back then, I simply wrote what I felt, found it helpful, and so kept doing it.

On the personal level, this is a story of persistence, commitment and survival. It is a story told largely from the inside out, with poetry reflecting my internal state of being and processing of that state, rather than offering much story. I have, however, included some reflective story around the period in which I wrote very little and was engaged in other artistic exploits.

I have always known, since I had the awareness to recognise it, that I experienced the world differently to those around me. I was painfully shy when young. I learned I was 'sensitive', 'stubborn', 'rebellious', 'weird'. Neurodivergence wasn't a common word if it even existed then, else I surely would have been diagnosed with some dysfunction or disorder.

Being sensitive in a harsh and desensitised world is not an easy thing, but it is not a disorder. It is a rebalancing of a humanity that has become wildly out of balance. It can feel like not making sense and can often mean struggling in a family that does not understand, and facing cultural norms and expectations that have harmful effects. It can sometimes feel like walking alone in the dark, not knowing where to go.

I composed this book as an offering of hope for any who, like me, experience or experienced deep struggle with physical, psychological or emotional wellbeing, with having a positive or stable sense of self, or with finding a feeling of belonging among others. It is for any who find a degree of resonance with even part of what is reflected in my early expressions.

May this book offer a thread of hope in times of darkness that there is another side beyond. May we find our way through to meet it.

# Phase 1: Distortion

I have had two major creative pursuits throughout my life; dancing, and the written word, most significantly in the form of poetry. From the age of 3, I danced classical ballet. I also played musical instruments as a child – piano, mostly, and cello, briefly.

I balleted my last at 13 years old. As that ended my life took a turn towards the difficult with the onset of intractable health problems that, in combination with environmental factors, left me physically exhausted and psychologically tormented. It was at that time that I started writing poetry as an expressive release.

I wrote my first of this type of poetry when I was 14. Not all of it survived through the years, and the order of writing was lost, with the exception of the very first claiming its rightful spot on the following page.

# Descent

I walk amid the darkness
What I seek I cannot find
And all I love and all I trust
I leave them far behind

Before me lays the path I tread
Around me the deep unknown
The souls of a forgotten world
They try to pull me down

Amidst broken rocks and fallen trees
The path goes winding on
And many smiling faces
I can see them far beyond

I reach out, I try to touch their hope
To find that they are gone

# Together

The rose withers and dies
The redness fades from the petals that wither
And bleed unto the skies

The black climbs down from the sky above
And devours all hope, all dreams and desires
Of happiness and love

I close my eyes and take your hand
And the fire comes and swallows the sun with hate
And we still stand

Together we shall fly away
Through the darkness out to the light we fly
And there we'll stay

# Enigma

I sleep with him
I sleep alone
I sleep with a lover
We sleep as one
But if I fall
I shatter
I am brittle
And lifeless
Forsaken
Yet shameless
Shaken
Still nameless
Unfound
And hiding
Unbound
Abiding

# Secret

As deep as the dark blue ocean
As wide as the winter sky
As high as a great mountain
I can fly

As soft as the wind's whisper
As cool as an autumn breeze
As warm as the sun in summer
It is real

As innocent as a new spring
As sweet as a fresh red rose
As dark as an eternal secret
Only I know

# Fool

Below me
As I swim in the darkness
Beside me
You sit with your heart in your mouth
Above me
I can see the sun rising
Your enchantment
Is my horizon

Catch me
I fall into your deep pool
Of overexposure
And indiscretion
Hide me
From the hurt and envy
Of a world of
Cruel obsession

Protect me
Beautiful you
Because cold confusion
Is not my colour
Fool me
As I look at you
And dream
That you are another

# With Love

In a war
I could kill you
And not know your name
In my mind
I could throw you
With no one to blame
With my hatred
You'd perish
And burn without flame
With my love
You would flourish
And I would the same

In a second
I could cut you
And take what I find
In a lifetime
I could move you
And follow behind
With my wrath
You would fail
And know yourself blind
With my love
You would know me
And I would not mind

In a game
I could beat you
And make you feel small

In your world
I could find you
And make you feel whole
With my scorn
You would crumble
And wither and fall
With my love
You would love
And that would be all

# Knowing

I know nothing
Don't try to tell me
I feel something
Based on simplicity

# Foe

Trust is a stranger
In your world of lies
Tell me you're honest
And truth then defy
Find pleasure in my failure
Deny me again
Jump the gun every time
But I win in the end

# Self-Hatred

Looking at you
I want you to die
Cold hard regret
I want you to cry
Hurt and confusion
I hate you so much
Pain and delusion
I recoil at your touch
Fuck you you bitch
So ugly so vile
Screw you you whore
I'm done with denial
Fuck you I hate you
Drown starve feel pain
Wither and dissolve
Into bitter rain
Fail, I detest you
I despair and I cry
I despise and I hate you
Why don't you just die

# Wrath

Come in
Smell the fire
Burning your flesh
With your own desire

Get out
Of my head
My senses to you
Are dead

Feel it
The coming of doom
Naked and unprotected
In an empty room

Run from it
Try to hide
But my wrath attacks
From inside

# Disarray

Fuck me
I hate you
I want you to cry
If you want to
Kill me
Don't care if I die
I lose myself
You find me
You scar me once more
Pain
Confusion
What is a heart for
Fuck me
You want me
You want me to cry
Hurt me
Abuse me
Then let me die
I crumble to dust
Scattered
In the wind
Spread me around
Hate me
Don't let me win

# Fiend

I abide in hell
The devil is my father
Cold hard eyes
Strong hard hands
A twisted mind
A powerful will
A word of ignorance
A delusion of love
He fills my cup
With acidic temperament
My closed thoughts
Are now wisdom
I know their ways
I follow behind
Study their paths
And triumph over all
I am Goddess of all
They never see me
But I breed in their minds
And devour their hope

# Fear

I know you but I don't understand you
I want you but I can't handle the change
I need you but I don't want to believe it
I love you but I can't risk the pain

My thoughts are confused, my heart contradicting
My feelings are strong like never before
My conscience repeating; be wary, be careful
Too scared I might lose you, too wise to want more

I can't stop the flood of emotions I'm feeling
Too late to protect the last standing tree
I tried not to let the waters envelop me
But I'm not as strong as I thought I could be

Don't interpret me wrongly, please don't turn your back
I'm lost and I'm wandering with nowhere to stay
Mist shrouds my path behind and before me
A little girl searching led farther astray

Confusion assails me destroys my last guard
My head is now reeling soaked in my own blood
I lay in the darkness awaiting a sign
Already in too deep, afraid to find love

# Bound

Reassure me
Confuse me
Take me over
Tell me love
Emotions pour
I run for cover
But oceans
Deep and blue
Swallow me whole
Gazing in
A breath of life
Then I fall
Catch me
Hold me
Keep me from you
Hold it up
Deny it
Fail to do
Fall apart
Pick me up
Keep me together
Tie my hands
Bind my love
Tell me never

# Loneliness

Empty heart
Lonely mind
Peace and love
None to find

Loneliness haunts me
Drives me astray
Depression consumes me
A little each day

Around me is beauty
Sickening grace
I look at myself
With scorn on my face

Around me is happiness
Hear them all laugh
I reach into myself
Lonely mind
Empty heart

# Being

The night is cold
The snow is falling
Clouds cross the sky
They cross my heart
Great dark fingers
Reach for my mind
My body is numb
Blackens my soul

I go outside
The wind is blowing
Branches break
They break my heart
Flash of lightning
Thunder roars
Drowns my sorrow
Destroys my soul

Why does winter always bring depression
Make hatred become the main obsession
I may just be trying to find my sanity
But it's hard to be
It's hard to be

# Captivity

Trapped, all alone
No place to escape to
Can't get out, cannot run
From this cruel conviction
Lying in darkness
Black shadows as friends
In my damp prison cell
Made of rules and restriction

I hear tales of happiness
Love and sunshine
Which contrast my delirious
Twisted illusions
I chip at the rock
Of my silent confinement
In solitude I reach
My lonely conclusions

I sit and I think
While my mind fills with sadness
Over the great misfortune
Of my separation
And I suffer alone
And I try to escape
From my damp prison cell
And my own desperation

# Fantasy

Throw myself into the river
I am never coming back
Colours fade, the whole world spins
In deathly shades of black
My blood flows with the water
Dilutes with my tears
I'll take your hatred with me
Drowning with my fears

The world will continue to live
The sun will continue to burn
The river will continue to flow
When I'm gone
The plants will continue to grow
Love will continue on
The earth will continue to turn
When I'm gone

Don't follow me down to the bottom
Don't tread my path of pain
Just remember me by the river
My tears when it rains
My blood on your fingers
My taste on your tongue
My touch in the lamplight
My warmth all winter long

You killed me from within
Scarred me without seeing
Tore my hopes apart
Killed my immortal being
The wind blows through my hair
As I think my last living thought
The river's calling to me now
My soul has been bought

The world will continue to live
The sun will continue to burn
The river will continue to flow
When I'm gone
The plants will continue to grow
Love will continue on
The earth will continue to turn
When I'm gone

# Sick

So sick of this ugliness that haunts me
So sick of never being put first
So sick of knowing this loneliness
So sick of feeling this feeling of hurt

I want to break out and just run away
But so many things tie me down
From every direction something pushing me further
Let it flow; I give up and drown

I look to you and feel sadness
I reach to you cos you're strong
I try to pull myself up to your level
Look for comfort in you but you're gone

I convince myself that you love me
I tell myself that you care
But I can't fool myself forever
I know you won't always be there

# Alienation

Feelings can be so empty
When there's no one to feel them for
When there's none to receive what you're giving
There's no point giving anymore

Hurt can run so deeply
When people just push you aside
When they forget that you also can suffer
When they forget that you are alive

Denial can be so dangerous
If you forget the truths of your world
If you choose to ignore the disappointments
And the burden of what is real

Loneliness can be so final
It can fill your mind with pain
And if you cannot overcome it
Then you will fail, and fail again

# Why

If good always triumphs over evil
Then why am I lagging behind
If the sun always rises after darkness
Then why is it still black as night
If love always conquers hatred
Then where has all your love gone
If friends always stick together
Then why do I feel so alone

# Infatuation

I can't believe I accepted these feelings
For someone so moody
So hard to predict
In a world that is twisted and life unadorned
It is too much
To say I admit
I wish to ignore you, I wish you to leave
You are my sickness, my pain
Strong and pure
What you drive from me is more than I have
Yet you are my prevention
My help and my cure
You have secured that my heart is now yours
Even though I resisted
And hard pushed you back
But failure I live with and weakness I gain
And the strength to turn away
Is the strength that I lack

# Contra

Trust from you is false
Faith will not be found in you
Security is a word unheard of
Love from you will not be true

Trust from me is dependable
Faith in me you will feel
Security is a word I know intimately
Love from me is real

Trust you will learn in time to come
Faith for this you will yearn
Security will become known to you
Love I will teach if you'll learn

# Nothing

There's nothing in me today
Nothing that fills me
Nothing that fuels me
I've nothing important to say
But nobody listens
To anything
Anyway

I've seen all I want of this world
All that is vicious
All that is pain
All that is hateful and cruel
But cries fade away
And disperse
On the wind

Calls for help fall on deaf ears
Answered by muted lips
Answered by empty hearts
I answer, I dry their tears
But nobody knows me
And as always
I find myself
Alone

# Turmoil

Can't think
Can't dream
Can't laugh
Can't cry
Overemotional
I don't know why
No understanding
No will to die
Nothing; no meaning
Stumbling I fall
Vacancies, all alone
No meaning at all

Words have no meaning
Man has no heart
Life is no comfort
I don't want to part
I don't want it ending
Not now, not yet
But I don't want to know you
I want to forget
You hurt me, you use me
You know I hate you
You want me, you lust me
I know that you do
Pain makes me stronger
I strive towards loss
I tear out my own heart
Ignoring the cost

Over and over
I claw at my skin
You know me, you like me
I won't let you in
I won't believe you
In shadows I crawl
You won't enter my heart
No meaning at all

Please don't turn away
Please understand
I don't expect love from you
Never I can
Take all that you want of me
I'll come at your call
You use me, I hate you
No meaning at all

Don't think, Don't dream
Don't laugh, don't cry
Don't use me, don't love me
Don't ask to know why
Accept me I pray to you
Me as I am
I'm not strong, I'm not you
I won't though I can
I cling to forgetfulness
Solitude my friend
Come make me happy
Make me smile again

No understanding
What do I say
I ask what to do
I ask every day
And every day onwards
Halfway I fall
Again and again
No meaning at all

# Moon

Love and hate like light and shadow
Exist together as one
But hate too often triumphs
Like the moon will replace the sun

I am the moon
I exist in darkness
Still shadows I can command
But when night is over
I falter
As the sun holds out his hand

He can take me wherever
And follow I will his lead
But love does not last
It dies
And with it my need

Once again I journey
My solitary nightly realm
And travel alone dark and worn
For my life one hope
One dream

That once again
The sun will shine
And shed his light on my face
And lift me from oblivion
Into everlasting grace

But it is only hope
Forever a dream
And it can never be
I am the moon
I exist in my darkness
And no one
Can touch
Me

# Despair

Why do I travel the hardest roads
Why do I climb the highest mountain
Why do I swim the longest river
Why do I face the strongest fountain
Why do I find the lowest valley
The widest crevice that I must cross
Why do I scale the steepest cliff face
The worst pain, the biggest loss

These are the questions I cannot answer
These are the deeds that I cannot do
But why do I want to make myself suffer
Why do I want to think I love you

# Insomnia

Night is too short
And daylight too swift
It fills the halls
With its rancid mockery
It laughs and it jests
While I turn my back
And cover my eyes
And cower
And hide
I just want to sleep

# Lost

I have no direction
I have lost my way
I can't find the trail
I followed day to day

Lost in a world
I don't understand
Clouded in mist
Pushed down by your hand

Trying to climb
Only to fall
The lowest I know
Nothing at all

Searching is fruitless
Discovery unkind
I dig deeper and deeper
To indulge in my mind

I swim in the darkness
I know and I love
From down here I watch
The people above

Depression
Denial
Anger
Revenge

Pain
Healing
Freedom
The end

# ?

Don't think as you feel
This is not real

# Phase 2: Adaptation

The next phase of my life involved little writing. I've offered some story accordingly. The beginning of the period was an incredibly difficult time, starting about halfway through my year of 20.

The pillars of my life during this phase otherwise were work (and study), travel and dance. It was a phase where I worked to adapt to the apparent circumstances of my existence. Within my circumstances though, I stretched and I grew, I sought and I questioned. I tried to live the life that was mine to live as best I could.

# The Whole World Up In Flames

Death

It was less than six months before my 21st birthday that he died. I had spoken to him on the phone the night before. He was surprised I recognised his voice from a simple 'hello'. Ridiculous man. I had known him since I was born, was I not to recognise the voice of one I knew so long and well?

Two days later I received the call that imploded my world. This great figure, gentle giant of the forest, centre of joyful childhood memories, was gone.

The night in between one call and the next, he was struck by a car, run over, dead in an instant. I was blissfully unaware at the moment the universe turned on its head. The idea that he could die was unthinkable. The loss of him was devastation, and the light of the world felt as though it had been snuffed out.

Miraculously, he was collected off the road and his body yet lived. Three days he lay in intensive care, long enough for those who loved him to visit and bid farewell, but no chance of survival.

I recall the moment I saw him that last time, the guttural sound that escaped me. As with when I first heard the news of the accident, my awareness sat behind and slightly above my head, the sound I made foreign to my ears, and detached from my awareness or governance.

There he lay, the big gentle man. But too short, his comical ginger hair gone all to white, his features swollen and misshapen. There was no life in that body. He was gone, and it was real.

The place where he died was on my regular route to university. For a time, the chalk outline remained where he fell, then it remained only in my mind. Six months later I started having panic attacks. At their worst they were happening on an hourly basis, and I didn't sleep for three days. I started on medication, which I remained on for over 10 years.

Somehow in this world gone mad, I had to live.

**Daddy Took Me To The Circus**

Endings

Two years after the death, my parents' marriage ended. I knew the night before my mum told me. We sat together in the lounge when my dad arrived home, and there was some interaction between he and my mother. It was not an unusual interaction on the surface, except somehow I knew it was the end.

I looked at my mum and she looked at me, and in a secret part of my mind I saw a tightly stretched rubber band finally snap.

It was not an easy separation, over the last months of my undergraduate degree. After dad eventually had left the house there was peace the likes of which I had never believed possible. It breaks my heart to think of it, but he was hell to live with, too often a whirlwind of rage and criticism and hypocrisy and judgement. Of pain. I found myself at the time with an insatiable anger towards him. I stopped seeing him.

A year after the separation, my dad was diagnosed with stage four cancer. A year later he died. In between was chaos, within and without. Conflict in the family, close and extended, and in it all the slow demise of my father while I yet seethed. How to meet a dying man with anger in my heart?

A time came when the anger faded to a background rumble and it was only then that I visited. I was glad that I waited. It was bittersweet, much better than all bitter, more honest than all sweet.

The night my dad died I sat on the kitchen floor, midnight approaching, cradling a bowl of just-cooked plain white rice, fingerfuls of which I placed in my mouth and chewed untasting. I was alone, as had become most comfortable for me, existing in a strange fugue state and unsure what else to do. But it felt cleaner than visiting his bedside one last time, given the familial discord.

The hospice called and told me he was gone. I wept as though my broken heart would never again be whole.

**Is That All There Is**

Work (and study)

By the end of my schooling my 'chronic fatigue' had reached its apex. I could barely make two full days in a row. My school made concessions without which I would not have been able to complete year 12. By the end of it I was beyond exhausted, even being told I looked green at one of my final assessments. I felt like the walking dead and looked it too.

I enrolled in university but deferred and took a gap year. After three months' rest I was somewhat recovered, and I found myself a part time administrative job. There, through the menial nature of the work, I found fresh conviction to pursue the path of higher studies the following year. That year of work afforded me the opportunity to rebuild my health and save money for my degree.

University was a breath of fresh air compared to learning in school, or to mundane work, and I felt myself greatly expand. I studied according to my interests in health (public health and psychology) with some philosophical electives. It all proved the foundation of the rest of my professional life (to date).

I worked in public health, population research and epidemiology for well over a decade. I was comfortable working with numbers and enjoyed data analysis and data collection, particularly the more creative human-centred elements. Yet I was routinely dissatisfied with the experience of work.

For all the expansiveness of university, work life felt like being shoved into a box, bits cut off that were deemed unnecessary or undesirable. This was more related to the culture of the workplace, which was most commonly emulated by managers rather than by colleagues and peers.

I had the unsettling and recurrent sense that I didn't fit, or that my skills and capabilities were coveted but not the whole person with which they came. I was somehow expected to be something other than what I was. As this was not possible, it meant workplaces and roles ended up being transient to some degree.

The longest I stayed, about six-and-a-half years, was in a job that did not feel that way. There, I felt growth personally as well as professionally, and I undertook a PhD. About halfway through my doctorate, leadership in the workplace changed and the culture started to shift as well. I was, yet again, in a place I did not fit. While I once envisaged a future in academia, I instead found myself again adrift and seeking.

That significant departure coincided with finishing my doctorate, mid- 30s approaching, and shortly after my interest turned back towards psychotherapy. I recommenced studying with the view to a change in profession, one where I could, perhaps, even work for myself. There was great appeal to the idea of no longer being buffeted about by detrimental workplace culture and egocentric management.

I felt burnt out on regular working life. I had enough examples, one after the other, that most work environments just weren't good for me. Even when I enjoyed the people, even when I enjoyed the work, something in me remained deeply and immutably unmet.

**If That's All There Is**

Travel

My first significant attempt to combat working life dissatisfaction during those years came in the form of travel, starting a couple of years after finishing university. Dad left me some money in his will, and at the same time several of my close friends were travelling overseas. I'd not thought actively about travel, but I found I had a desire to see different lands.

The first time I travelled, I spent three months in Europe. On the other side of the world from all I'd ever known, it was a revelation. For a few years, I saved all year for a big trip away, and in doing so I discovered hidden parts of myself; more capable, more competent, and luckier than I'd ever appreciated. I stretched my cage, and within it, I grew.

Yet between travels still festered this discontent. And questions started to arise. Was this really what life was? What it was supposed to be? By all standard measures, I was doing well but inside I didn't feel it. I drank too much. I partied with my friends on weekends, centering my hopes for finding fulfilment on these temporary escapes, expecting something to happen, though what I don't know. I was looking for something. But dissatisfaction, exhaustion, disillusionment, dejection, were all too common players in my mental space.

I started to wonder; why was this even considered a normal or expected way to live one's life? What would it look like to feel happier all the time, not just when on holiday? A few weeks of freedom a year, bought by a lifetime of servitude for some externally contrived purpose. It seemed somewhat insane, with no real sense of meaning in it at all. I started to consider what living a truly good life might mean for me.

**Then Let's Keep Dancing**

Then entered the other major part of this phase and a long love; the return of dance.

I first engaged with partnered dancing in my early 20s, though only briefly. In my late 20s, I found my way back and this time it stuck. I was actively engaged in it for about 15 years, primarily in Blues dance but otherwise vintage swing styles, with an exploration of various styles throughout. My travelling aspirations became more localised as I regularly attended dance events around Australia.

Here I experienced something entirely new, a new awareness, and a new understanding of dialogue. I in fact learned an entire new language, though it was only years later I thought of it this way. It taught me to perceive different levels of communication. I also developed a new appreciation for subtle roles in communication and the influence of power imbalance, which existed between roles, between genders, and according to social capital within the dance world. Often inconvenient to acknowledge for those in positions of power and influence, it was too commonly left unchecked.

Notably, I experienced the unrivalled bliss of synchronous shared movement. I would say I was addicted to it in those early days. Exercise releases endorphins, associated with pleasure and pain relief. Physical connection, as in a close dance like Blues, releases oxytocin, relieving anxiety and depression and engendering feelings of trust and closeness. A potent combination.

As with any state-altering substances, whether externally applied or internally generated, it creates vulnerability; especially within those who have struggled to feel such things in their life. Dance tended to attract these individuals. Vulnerability in turn creates an inviting environment for those with nefarious intent, who can capitalise on entrenched power imbalances to serve their own ends. Dance attracted these individuals as well.

## *Caged*

The caged bird sings
A song I understand
Of a time when he will fly
About all the land

He sings of a life
Beyond his iron bars
He sings of breathing sweet clear air
And sleeping beneath the stars

He sings of seeing the far horizon
Push up the sun each morn
And at eve dragging it down
To again prepare for dawn

I listen to his song of joy
He sings his song to me
And together we dream yet both do know
That we can never be free

# Home

Lead me home
I'm lost
I cannot find my way
I wonder what's the use
Of this day to day
I want somebody to love me
I don't want to be alone
Please won't you lead me home

Lead me home
I'm lost
Beneath the pale white moon
The world is full of shadows
In this evening gloom
I want something to believe in
But I find my faith is gone
Please won't you lead me home

Lead me home
The grass is red
The sky turns black
The heavens spill their frozen tears
Upon my loaded back
I need someone to trust in
But my heart is heavy so
Please won't you lead me home

Lead me home
My eyes are closed
They open wide
I look around and so I find
It's not so dark outside
There's somebody who loves me
There's no need to be alone
Please won't you take me home

# Bitter Pill

Undermine
As I look at you
Overtime
My mind working through
I keep my feelings hidden
But you can see me thinking
Behind
Trust in me
You would be a fool
Refuse me
I'm all over you
You know you can choose to take my tainted words
Or find the truth

You run
But you can't get far away
You try
But you feel you've got to stay
You think
But your heart controls your head
You know
You should swallow me instead
And I fool you

Honestly
You may think you need me
Openly
Choke on naivety
Honey I will take you over
Baby I will make you think it's
Alright

Can't you taste the bittersweet of confusion
While you swim safely locked in your own delusion
And I scream
But you won't let me out
And I shake
But you know it's about
The only thing that I can do
Against you

You turn
But too late to ever know
You hope
But it's still too far to go
You feel
But your mind's already dead
You're lost
So you'll swallow me instead
And I fool you

# Breaking

Now the day is over
Let me grieve again
While hope shone with the sun
I could feel no pain

Now darkness falls upon me
My heart it bleeds once more
Because I've lost my lover
And it cuts me to the core

My power for good is waning
My will gives way to sorrow
Tonight, I grieve
Tonight, love fails
But I'll look for the sun tomorrow

## Abuse

I was so free and strong and beautiful
I was kind and open and loving
I wanted to love and be loved
I wanted to express and be accepted
My whole being, my whole heart
My soul and spirit
All of me
I was

I was patient and forgiving
I was giving and generous
I gave all I could

I was hurt and misled
I was damaged I was broken
I was fooled and felt foolish
I was wronged and felt wrong
I became doubt and worry and closed and afraid
I became alone and old and dusty and worn
I became a stranger
Someone else in the mirror
Someone else in someone else's skin
I lost me, I lost my future
I lost my hope for a better tomorrow

I was burned
But the flames failed to burn me all away
My heart, my core, my tender spirit
Remained
Charred
But inside green and full of all the life
You thought you had destroyed

# Capital

Wind over Capital Hill
Forty-four naked flag poles
Rattling like corpses bones

# The Way She Feels

A few years into my dancing in earnest, about halfway through this second phase, the international vintage dance scene was rocked by accusations of sexual assault and abuse committed by high profile instructors and organisers. I had my own firsthand experience of the same in Australia.

How I perceived it upon later reflection is that the potent blend of power imbalance and organic intoxication had inevitably erupted. The response to the crisis ranged from vigorous support to rabid rejection. There appeared to be an inverted association between need and action; spaces which had more entrenched issues were often the least willing to adopt change or acknowledge the need for it.

My positive perception of the dance community was damaged and never entirely recovered, not just from the occurrences themselves, but from what appeared to be an embedded complacency in the face of such gross injustice. Broadly, with limited exception, action tended to lean towards the superficial and reactionary and overlooked the deeper drives underpinning harmful conduct, even among the supportive crowd.

As I was not ready to give up dancing, I took the approach of engaging with different dance communities often for relatively brief periods of time. This led to exploration of multiple styles and expanded creativity, which I loved, but also to remaining reasonably detached from any community.

I credit my long-term connection to Blues dance to the emergence of a subgroup within the community, largely driven by queer and feminist culture. I involved myself in event organisation with likeminded others for a few years, in which we centred principles of culture, safety, and respect, and ran as more community- and peer-led projects. It felt inspired and purposeful.

Then COVID hit, and it all ground to a halt along with so much else. I suppose in the eagerness to restart dance it was easy to dismiss those hard-won commitments to safety and respect. Caring people had always tended to self-select out of uncaring environments. Even at the best of times, given a revolving door of unsuspecting incomers, it was easy for uncaring spaces to persist just through paying lip service. Paired with the post-lockdown back-to-normal-at-all-costs attitude, I guess it didn't really stand a chance.

So came a sense of regression, progress unmade, complacency back in force, the sub-community disintegrated, and my inspiration started to dim. In time, not seeing what I wanted to be involved in reflected anywhere outside of my own efforts, the grip of my once-relentless passion found there was nothing left to hold on to. Slowly, and not entirely willingly, I let go.

I learned a lot through dance. Of certain, dance reflected the very same issues as present in any other hierarchical, patriarchal, and egocentric power structure. The desire for personal significance and power tends to go hand in hand with a deep aversion to genuine personal responsibility and accountability. Indeed, the places where it is most needed, the capacity for honest self-reflection is generally most lacking.

But dance itself, as a practice, was one of the best things I have ever done. I learned many positive and beneficial lessons beyond simply the skill itself. Above all it brought a great joy into my life not previously known.

# Phase 3: Activation

The return of poetry into my life was accompanied by the completion of my training as a holistic counsellor and psychotherapist, which coincided with the COVID pandemic and my gradual withdrawal from dance. Over the course of a few short years, I experienced a series of personal events, a change in career, and dramatic internal shifts, set against the oft-chaotic global background.

# Wind

Watch the wind
It blows
It moves
It moves the leaves
The branches sway

Hear the wind
It sighs
It sings
It speaks softly of softness and light

Feel the wind
It breathes onto me
Into me
It fills me and soothes me

And like the leaves I am moved
Like the sound I soften
I exhale
A little wind
On into the world

# Dawn chill

The rising sun, unseen,
Icy pinpricks sear my skin
Stillness, consume me

# Heavy

Walking a path alone
Behind me a menacing tread
Each stride sending a shockwave
Out into the surrounding peace
As though he must stamp his mark
On every patch of earth he passes over
Must leave an impression, deep and lasting
Not realising that the next rain
Will wash him clean away

The energy in forming that heavy foot
Energy denied from other movement
The swinging of arms
The motion forward
A needed change in direction
Energy so concentrated in the
Downwards
Stamp
In every pace

Better it may be
To take a lighter step
Keep energy free
For running dancing weaving
Making a path your own with every movement
Through subtlety and ease
Even if all that's left of your passing
Is a soft scent
And a subtle breeze

# Contemplations on a Leaf

Everyday
I climb a mountain
Sometimes under bright sun
Sometimes under cloud
Sometimes with drops of water in my hair and eyes

Today the path is muddy
Always there is mud after a deluge
Mist blocks my view in all directions
Yet I see clearly
Not the far distance

But one leaf of pastel rainbow
Bearing drops of the night's rain
Delicate colours, stark in the surrounding drabness
It's gentle grace
Calls me to remember
What I am here for
Who I choose to be
Why it is important

Everyday I climb a mountain
I meet a new me waiting at the peak
I bid loving farewell to the me of yesterday
And every day it is easier than the day before

# Imbalance

Codependence
Is fear masquerading
As love
It doesn't feed the soul
But picks at it
Slowly eroding
Vital energy
It feels
Sad and weary
Heavy and wanting
Empty and bottomless
Over time
It grows towards
The loss
It seeks to avoid

# As Within So Without

I close my eyes
And listen to the sounds
Of nature around me
In the wilderness
On a narrow track
In solitude and silence
I open my eyes
And my focus is drawn
Not by a tree, or bird
Or rustle in the undergrowth
But by the movement
Reflected on the inside of my sunglasses
A single strand of my hair
Vibrating in the cool gentle breeze
Lit gold by a caught ray of the sun
Amongst all the splendour of nature
My attention is captured by
A reflection
Of a part
Of my Self

# The Meeting Tree

On a walk through the wilds in quiet solitude
I turn from my path towards a short detour
At the end of the track the ground drops away
Into a great gorge
An expanse of space between where I stand
And the wilderness on the other side
In my mind I know you stand there
On that far terrain
The details of your surrounds concealed
By bush and tree and fold in earth and rock
I imagine on a clear calm day
Our voices could carry across the space
And we could each hear the other call
Feel a connection despite the distance
Yet even as this thought arises
A great wind comes flying from the east
Tearing through the gorge
My eyes captivated by its invisible passage
My ears filled with the violence of its roar
It rises with a seemingly perpetual crescendo
I remain a moment longer, withstanding
Before I retreat from the chill of it
Back to my path.

As I continue, I see the other side
Your land
Drawing closer with the narrowing of the gorge
I recall another path I once followed
That leads to that far side where you yet stand in my mind

Across a creek sometimes swollen and impassable
A beautiful journey to a beautiful view
A cul-de-sac of delight
No onward journey
Only another inevitable departure
I see there is a place where paths meet
Yours and Mine
A place where possibilities are birthed
New ways lay in wait to be discovered
Futures spring and dance in the air
Spectres longing also to be grasped and realised
Someday I may reach that place
And find you there
Under the meeting tree
Maybe I will pass it many times
Until one day I find your path overgrown and untrodden
Closed off from its lack of use
Our possible reconnection forever lost

For now, I simply continue
Following my path
The way I know will take me home
And in a quiet secret part of my soul a voice whispers

May the spectral futures dance
At the place where our paths converge
Under the meeting tree
Where we can See each other
Face to face, Eye to Eye
Where we can Hear each other's words
No matter how subtly spoken
No matter how the wind keeps blowing

# Climbing Mountains

When climbing a mountain
Don't look towards the top of the path
Don't look at how much more work you have to do
Look only at the ground in front of you
At where you must next place your feet
Focus on each step you are taking
And when you feel the need to rest
Turn your back on the journey upwards
Leave closed the door to being disheartened
Look instead on how far you've come
When you only focus on each next step
You will always be surprised
By how much progress you've made
Times of rest and reflection are important
So you can appreciate the work you have done
To come so far
Stopping doesn't mean
You've forgotten the destination
That you've given up on the mountain
It gives you time to honour your efforts
Your resilience, your unwavering heart
To rekindle the fire that burns
For you to meet the summit
And know in every part of your being
That you are worthy of its grand views

# The Unbound Woman

I am not here to amuse you
To dance for you
To distract you from your suffering
To draw you from your stubborn self

I was not made to be yours
To belong to anyone or anywhere
I belong everywhere and nowhere
Made for everyone and no one

I did not become to save you
I do not bring coaxing words
My hands may comfort
But they do not carry

I have not walked
A path of fire
To wallow in your pools
Nor seek permission to burn

I stand
Upon my own feet
Supported by the hands
Of unseen thousands

The only person
Who can choose your way
Who can walk your path
Is you

Come with your eyes open  
A light on your brow  
Your heart in your mouth  
Or do not come at all

# Unrequited

He said
Fall for me
See me as I wish to be seen
Want me so badly
That you forget who you are
Abandon yourself
So that all you have to rely on
Is me and my opinion
Betray yourself
Surrender your authority
To serve me and mine
Only then will I love you
When you are so hobbled
You can never leave me
He said
Fall
Throw yourself on my altar
And I will cut you to suit my mood

She said
Rise for me
See me for who I am
Feel me so deeply
That you remember who you are
Recall your strength
Gather your energy
Bring yourself to your feet
Bear yourself with integrity
Hold your heart with care

So that you can offer me
A safe place to be soft
A warm place to lay myself bare
A home to infuse with my love
She said
Rise
Stand beside me
That we may create heaven on earth

He said
Rising
Is too hard
I will not relinquish my hell
In fear of not reaching your heaven

She said
Falling
Is too easy
I will not relinquish my heaven
In certainty of reaching your hell

# As I Breathe

Sometimes
A weight rests down on me
And all my swirling moving
Becomes still and stuck
Frozen
I am both restless and flattened
The moving wanting to move
The resistance exhausts
Collapse
The only flow I have
Is the water of my body
Out the corners of my eyes
Resting
As it runs its course
Weaving through my being
Clearing dirt and stones
Release
The weight withdraws
Rising as I rise once more
Relearning to stand
Sometimes
I forget that to be human
Is to feel as I breathe
In. Out. And let go.

# Broken Things

I found you lying in the sand
Your marred form calling to me
Mirroring the worn feeling of my heart
As I walked the sunny shore
All sorrow darkening inside

Now I think to leave you
Resting on the broken branch
Of a tree that once spoke to me
Of love and tenderness
Since fallen rendered

I observe you anew
As I carry you to your resting place
Far from the sunny gloomy shore
Thinking to leave you alone and forlorn
To echo the long-closed journey of my love

You rest in my hand
Worn by life's pressures
The constant moving wearing
Missing pieces like living loss
Like the embodiment of grief

No more a thing of perfect form
Bearing the marks of time
And the interminable shifting of matter
Your spaces yearning creating
An ethereal beauty

And I decide I will keep you
I will hold you against the wearing of the world
And with me you shall be whole
For that is your countenance
In my eyes

# On Waiting

They say patience is a virtue
Often too a struggle
In this world of pace and driving and striving
Sometimes waiting comes regardless
Seeking patience
A pause between, a not knowing
As a subtle tension materialises
And slowly builds

Like sitting in the pouch of a slingshot
Imperceptibly stretched tighter, taughter
Felt through an excruciating formless restlessness
A roiling in the discomfort of the unchanging

Until the direction of change reveals itself
And there comes the propulsion, ready or not
No room for hesitation
No space to doubt
There is simply movement, racing towards the new
Meeting the desire for relief
The different
Change

Maybe the waiting is brief maybe long
Intense or mild
The inevitable movement proves
That the deeper the waiting the tenser the tension
The greater the change for which you are prepared
And the newer the new that is yours

Swirling in the beyond
Until you arrive

But first
There must be discomfort
In the waiting

# Avoidant

Some day you may meet someone
And think they offer a meal
Something satisfying of substance
Only to find not even a snack
Not even a mouthful
Not even a pastry puff full of air

You find instead a trail of crumbs
And you follow
To seek the end of the trail
Even as the light fades
But all there is, is an endless trail
And an illusory scatterer

A person of flight and fancy
With games of push and pull
Come and go
Hot and cold
Steeped in the fear of your coming
Close enough to see
They carry naught but crumbs

Too close and crumbs become stones
Thrown from those they have piled around
Their inaccessible heart
Even though they so want you to reach it
Crumbs and stones the tools
To keep you trapped and wanting, controlled

No matter what they do or say or want
No matter how long you play
Their games of push and pull
Come and go hot and cold
Love cannot enter a closed door
Love cannot pass through a wall of stones

You learn to see breadcrumbs for what they are
A beggar's bowl
Bottomless and ever hungry
A person offering crumbs
Only has crumbs to offer
Such a one will consume you instead of feed you

Hoping the promise of crumbs
Will be enough
To keep you bound
A promise that will never be realised
A promise you must accept
Or get nothing at all

Sweetheart, choose nothing
For an unkept promise is nothing too
Let them alone with their dwindling crumbs
Let them live what they choose
So giving them too
A chance to choose anew

Do not sit and wait at a closed door
Don't settle for less than subsistence
When you are worthy of a feast
Learn to bake your own bread
Unless you are offered
The whole damn bakery

# The Loving Void

As a child I screamed
Walking into the kitchen
My tiny toddling form
With strong grown lungs
Set forth such a cry
I don't know why
But I can imagine
The calm veneer
Of a household evening
Overlaying a shattered heart
An empty deceitful peace
No safety no stability
A constant cooing threat
An ominous hum

In my child's terror
Hands took me pulled me
Into a small dark room
And closed the door
Alone staring at the distorted night
It entered around me
Holding me silent
My wide eyes gulping
At the loving void
Taking in from exile
What was not elsewhere found
A comfort and a calm
The gentle caress
Of black solitude

No wonder I seek
Isolation for solace
And oblivious disconnection
As cherished companion
Of all those I encountered then
They loved me best
So I learned that the void
The space between
Where all you have is what you bring
Yourself
Is not to be feared
But stood within, open
Receptive to the peace
Of self-dissolution

# Madness

Women are shamed for their madness
The madness of women
The uncontrolled emotion the hysteria
The lying in bed unable to rise weeping into pillows
The guttural scream of despair to the sky
The gnashing of teeth, the pulling of hair
The rending of clothes, of flesh
The primal rage
Of being misunderstood unseen unmet
And the crushing pressure of an expectant world becomes too much
For the mind and heart to bear in silence
A madness of feeling
Writ in expression
The soul trying to break free

But what of the madness of men?
Where is that spoken?

The madness that severs men from their own heart
To dance instead to the beat of a mechanical clock
Calling their life's end nigh from the moment of their birth
Reminding him that time can run out in a moment
And before then he must make is presence felt
He must matter and all must know it
Stamp his print deep into the earth
And that mark be marvelled and adored
Without that, the thudding grind ever grating
A tick tock telling he is not yet enough
As though that has more gravity than the pulse of life

More pull than a warm embrace
More significance than love

The madness that urges a man to forsake all feeling
In favour of empty glasses and emptier words
And fear
The fear of being seen in any way as weak or unknowing
When no man taught them how to be anything other
When no man showed them anything other could exist
To act certain while mired in uncertainty
To act confident while seething with worthlessness
To imagine strength as dominance over
Rather than support and holding of
To display this weak strength as a badge of honour
While the child inside weeps and wails
Dismissed abandoned unloved

The madness that leads a man to beat his own child
Whether with words or fists so long as they are down and cowering
A testament to his great weak strength
That leads a man to beat his wife a woman he may claim to love
But how can one know love when their heart is a husk
So deprived of sustenance
So beaten first within himself
The constant vehement defence of a shell so brittle
That the smallest slight can crack it all to pieces
And he dissolves in his madness and his fury
Destroying any who stand close enough to touch

The madness that leads a man to commit atrocities
Of rape or murder or war or genocide
Repression and destruction
Of that which threatens this weak strong man's
Illusion of control

Cruelties unimaginable against the innocent
Against the very planet we depend on
And her pure creatures
Factory farms and factory foods
All reduced to consumable things
No longer bearers of sacred energy
Nourishment from the Great Mother
Yet how often do we hear and see and live this
How often repeated day by day, year by year, decade by decade
Again and yet again
Does making these things common
Render them sane?

Men are lauded for their madness
Made leaders and made rich
Set on thrones of cold hard stone
Atop mighty towers of cold hard steel
Hating anyone who may rest in softness
Or offer it to others
Or be other in any way
A prime minister, a president
A priest, a king, a CEO
A boss, a father, a man on the street
A tyrant, any one
A madness of belief
Writ in oppression
The ego desperate to survive

What of the madness of men
The insanity of not knowing how to feel
The insanity of believing that being unfeeling uncaring disconnected
Inhumane
Is a superior form of humanity

# Serious

I fear I have become a serious person
Where once I sought to laugh and smile
I now seek the quiet and the still
The solemn and sincere
What little of that is here
Living in the world of men
The only true lightness I find
Lies outside
In the bush by the shore on the mountain or the hilltop

Among men there is no care
Vacant minds and hot air
Time passed and life spent
As though nothing it meant
But shallow pleasure
False smiles and knives concealed
False smiles that hurt as much as knives
More
Because they lie so deadly sweet

So I am
Serious as I can be
Wanting to feel and being free
In this cold and crass unfeeling place
Even though as I do and I face
In my heart a reservoir of pain
That I cry again and again

Yet even as it hurts it feels good
Because it is real and it should
Like the bush the shore the mountain and hill
We live to hurt and we live to heal
We live to cry we live to feel
We live to live a life that is real
Not cold and careless and hollow and absent
But warm loving full present
And when that is not outside to be found
I go inside where it abounds
The beat of my heart
The cacophony of subtle rhythm
Singing through my living body

I am serious
But I turn inside and there I dance
The dance of life

# Not Sorry

"I'm sorry", she said
And I replied, "you're 'right"
Her apology given as we approach one another on a walking track
A narrow track but not that narrow
Wide enough for two to pass
Barely breaking stride, a slight turn of the body to make room
I make room, it causes me no trouble at all
Yet she is sorry
For nothing more than being in that place at that time
That I must make a small adjustment in my movement
To accommodate her existence
Well may I ask why but of course I already know
The dynamic learned, too often as a child
That they can never be wrong, or rather
That you can never be right if your right means they are wrong
You are only allowed to be right when it is no inconvenience to them
First and foremost comes their comfort
And you must cater, ever, to serve that goal
Even if it means that you must learn that you are wrong
And can only ever be right by their approval
Their approval, ever set just beyond your reach, because it is not yours
It is theirs, and to keep it so, you must never have it
Were you to defy them and deny them their comfort, what do they do?
You say they are being unfair, they become more prejudiced
You say they didn't listen, they deny you ever spoke
You say you cannot relate with them, they attack your self-worth
They respond to your defiance of their rightness
By proving you right
"I'm sorry", she said

The sorry she is still owed and will never receive
The sorry she was taught to live, now given without thought, without cause
And I replied, "your right"

# Warble

Birds sing for the joy of the day
No more quintessential sound
Than the magpie atop a metal light pole
Singing his joy
Singing his heart across the streetscape
The paved over wooded paths
The ghosts of trees long gone
The levelled rise and fall
Of a natural landscape
The buried streams
The lost dreams

In the manmade artifice
He sings
Of the truth that still rests beneath
The natural balance of the universe
In the darkness you find your light
In emptiness you find peace
In your destruction you find rebirth
In the losing you find your Self

You cannot know joy when in fear of sorrow
Pleasure in fear of pain
Wisdom in fear of ignorance
Love in fear of the grief of loss

If you refuse to die
You will not know how it feels
To truly live

If you refuse to face the demons
That prowl the depths of your psyche
You will not receive their gift
And find your path to freedom

When you fall into darkness
If you refuse to open your eyes
You will not see the light
That guides you home

Open your eyes
My love
Open your eyes

# When She Calls

Some days I awaken
Unsettled and shaken
And I know it is not a day like any other
But a day for retreat
A day on which I need rest but more
I need the serene
I need the green world
Away from any artificial edifice

To be
Where the wind sighs in endless murmur
Branches careen in endless dance
Water calls in endless song
She sings
Peace, darling
Let me hold you awhile
Let me remind you what is real
And who you are

You are
A child of nature
A child of the stars
A weaver of magic
A spinner of dreams
You answer to no one
But the wisdom of the Cosmos
And she says
Life dances in you
The earth lives through you

The world reflects and amplifies you
A tiny perfect fractal
Of the unified whole

You are the living breath
Of a boundless Universe
A ripple of the ceaseless wave
From which springs all Creation
An exhale of Eternity
Fanning the spark of awareness
That yet lives in all
Lie still for a moment
Breathe
Be

# Darkness

My mind scattered
Fleeing from what tries to hold it
In panic it darts
In pain it screams
It cannot be caught
In that vice-like grip, a claw
Of shadow and dark
But in its escape
It flees into jaws of terror
Worse than shadow
Darker than dark
In that perilous place
A quiet voice speaks
Do not fear the darkness
For it is but an apparition
Just air
Space unilluminated
Shine upon it a single beam
And it is gone

# Awaken

              I awoke one morning
           To a strangeness in my head
       Something that called clear to me
            As I lay upon my bed
         Words spoken soft and quiet
       Though it was no earthly voice
      It laid before me two clear paths
           Two realities; a choice
         One path worn and trodden
        Well followed and well known
     The other unclear confused obscured
          That I must forge alone
       Then that voice it spoke once more
         Though not a single word
          Inside a verity revealed
          But felt rather than heard
          Followed then a question
       "Will you accept?" gently said
     Before my answer I dreamed myself
         Along each path to tread

Your truth makes me unsteady
The ground beneath me shakes
And a worry begins to rapid rise
When my foundation quakes
The well-worn road it looks so clear
I see where each step should fall
There's nothing unexpected here
No real surprise at all

Though maybe nothing truly good
Some jollity, fleeting thin
That brings a temporary relief but
Can never breach the skin
The same it may be day after day
But the familiar feels just fine
I accept the world as I am told
Fix my gaze and dull my mind
I let my youthful dreams dissolve
I let my hopes fall by
I nod my head and don a smile
And how the years they fly
I repeat the patterns I was taught
Discomfort I assuage
I may not be truly happy
But I feel safe within my cage
If I were to believe your truth
The things that it would mean
Of all I'd see I'd overlooked
Let pass unknown, unseen
The pain I caused to those I loved
Through ignorance and fear
A poison dram, a bitter pill
It will not enter here

The truth you speak offends me
And rattles my world's core
I trust only what I've ever known
Of those that came before
Recognition threatens suffering
And I will not wear the cost
It's painful to remember
When it shows all I have lost

So I remain 'stead stubborn
With blinkers by my eyes
I will not look t'wards any truth
That sits outside my lies
My mind may run in circles
But I know the rutted track
And if I ever were to leave it
I'd never find my long way back
What's in the unknown spaces
Looks dark from where I stand
With no assurances that way
I'll stay on known land

"No thank you" mumbled weakly
When I finally did speak
I settled in I turned my back
And swiftly fell to sleep

Your truth it makes me curious
My tethers all fly free
I do not know where I belong
Or how I'm meant to be
The way I thought that I would go
It fades and drifts away
It makes no sense to follow still
Where I walked day to day
Each step is now uncertain
I must trust a different part
Of Self that speaks less in the mind
More from within the heart

Your truth calls me against the grain
The familiar and the safe
When one cannot see what lies ahead
One must rely on faith
All becomes turned inside out
What once was up goes down
Should I try and walk with what was
I find it's turned around
And while I reel from all the change
There's something growing strong
Something within that I had lost
Yet known all along

I perceive myself all fresh anew
And nothing do I lack
In the mirror I see I am much more
Than what's reflected back
I feel a stirring hope within
It echoes the truth you speak
It sends a light where I am dark
Strength where I am weak
And when I break it holds me close
Supports me when I stumble
As all I held in truth before
Cannot help but wholly crumble
See my towers are all broken now
My walls are torn apart
I can no more bear the heavy shield
That hid my yearning heart
All tender raw I am laid bare
My nerves are all aflame
Yet agony greater it would be
To hide my Self again

I'll walk into the wild unknown
This journey I'll begin
Though it may mean I first accept
I know not any thing
And whither does it lead me
This untrod path alone
Though I cannot see I surely feel
That I am coming home

"Yes please" I spoke in wonder
Though my voice did slightly shake
I sat and Saw with eyes wide bright
When first I true did wake

# First Light

There is poetry in the unfettered bush
In the sun in the breeze
In the grass in the leaves
In the bushes and the trees
Furry body scurrying feet
Singing songs and dreaming dreams
Weaving story preaching peace
Walk a while let your tired heart ease
Your soul rest your spirit breathe

# *Catalyst*

Out of nowhere it came, I might say when feeling in a light and casual mood. But it wasn't from nowhere, it was timed so precisely, and I had been prepared…

…though I knew it not.

My therapeutic training, exploring perception of the imperceptible; attending shamanic and mystical workshops; and a small few odd, liminal experiences in the preceding months…

A few weeks prior I had the bizarre feeling that a switch within me had been flicked on, and I was lit up like a beacon, signalling my presence but by and to what or whom, for why…

…I knew it not.

I lived those weeks in a gentle high, no fear seemed to touch me, I was unassailable; a feeling which sat deep within me, undeniable. I revelled in it, so starkly different from the state I had known most of my life…

A state in which I was required to be, else I would have given him none of my time nor attention…

Several months earlier we had met. He pulled on my attention in an unusual way, and so I observed him from the edge of my perception; 'player', 'shallow', 'capricious', what interest in such as that…

I found a clear and resounding 'no', that grabbed that tenuous thread of attention and pulled it down into my subconscious spaces and there it lodged, resolute…

Until…

This strange, suspended state enveloped me, a state outside of the normal bounds of reality, outside of time. Kairos instead of Chronos. Mythos instead of Logos. A message arrived boldly in my inbox and instead of 'no' I met curiosity, but of what…

…I knew it not.

Magic blossomed alive in my veins, singing to me in a way I'd not before heard. It sang with and around him. The very air between us flared to life, electricity sparked in our fingertips and the world around fell to a pale murmur…

Kairos flooded in, overtaking; I knew I could fall into his presence and feel held in a way I had never previously known was possible. An energy of such intense Love lay already waiting, irrationally unnervingly intense, we just had to tap its vein...

One night, before Chronos again reared sovereign, and I still stood in Kairos, while he in terror fled…

…though I knew it not.

The dawning realisation that Truth did not match reality, the gulf between yawned and swallowed me whole, the stark contrasting contradiction a blow of such a magnitude it near scattered me to the corners…

The beacon light fled from my grasping fingers, but something else had been lit; a dark flame, leading me down into the deepest darkest underworld, and three months of intense agony…

There are words I could put to that experience, but they would sound like madness. Perhaps it was…

Perhaps the only exit out of an insane world is by way of what that world would label insanity…

My entire existence turned round and upside down on the nexus of one fateful night…

Yet through it all I met something miraculous; a sense of Self beyond self. What had previously been only hopeful intellectual became visceral…

The knowledge that we are human, and we are Soul…

Both are meaningful. Both matter. We are a miraculous congruence of the disparate. A dance of material and immaterial, finite and infinite, matter and spirit…

A cosm beyond this material world exists in truth…

…though we may know it not.

We have become lost, because we have forgotten.

But we can remember.

# Still Water

I go down to the water and my mind falls still
No thought can enter in
I went with the intent to write
On the most significant of things

Yet as I gaze upon the surface calm
The soft breeze strokes my hair
The sun is warm, the shade is cool
There's nought else in the air

No thoughts to grasp, no idea calls
No terror stalks the ground
And as my tension slow dissolves
The wide blue sky smiles down

The weary earth she smiles back
As she cradles me with love
The joy she feels when I visit with her
Mother Earth below, Father Sky above

And I receive their ever-gentle reminder
That though I may walk alone
I can always come where the sky smiles wide
To their eternal 'welcome home'